FREAKY FREELOADERS
BUGS THAT FEED ON PEOPLE

BEDBUGS

JOYCE JEFFRIES

PowerKiDS press.

New York

Published in 2016 by The Rosen Publishing Group, Inc.
29 East 21st Street, New York, NY 10010

First Edition

Editor: Katie Kawa
Book Design: Michael J. Flynn

Photo Credits: Cover (bedbug) smuay/Shutterstock.com; cover, pp. 3–24 (frame) Dinga/Shutterstock.com; pp. 4, 6, 9 (adult bedbug), 10, 14, 16, 18, 20 Marco Uliana/Shutterstock.com; p. 5 Roger Eritja/Oxford Scientific/Getty Images; p. 7 jareynolds/Shutterstock.com; p. 8 louento.pix/www.flickr.com/photos/lou_bugs_pix/5424454836/CC BY-ND 2.0; p. 9 (nymph) Nigel Cattlin/Visuals Unlimited/Getty Images; p. 11 iStock/Thinkstock.com; p. 12 louento.pix/www.flickr.com/photos/lou_bugs_pix/3104690663/CC BY-ND 2.0; p. 13 Stan Honda/AFP/Getty Images; p. 15 Darlyne A. Murawski/National Geographic/Getty Images; p. 17 jcarillet/E+/Getty Images; p. 19 louento.pix/www.flickr.com/photos/lou_bugs_pix/324802634/CC BY-ND 2.0; p. 21 Carlos Osorio/Toronto Star/Getty Images; p. 22 U.S. Department of Agriculture/www.flickr.com/photos/usdagov/15257458553/CC BY-ND 2.0.

Library of Congress Cataloging-in-Publication Data

Jeffries, Joyce, author.
 Bedbugs / Joyce Jeffries.
     pages cm. — (Freaky freeloaders: Bugs that feed on people)
 Includes bibliographical references and index.
 ISBN 978-1-4994-0742-6 (pbk.)
 ISBN 978-1-4994-0745-7 (6 pack)
 ISBN 978-1-4994-0746-4 (library binding)
 1. Bedbugs—Juvenile literature. I. Title. II. Series: Freaky freeloaders. Bugs that feed on people.
 QL523.C6J44 2015
 595.7'54—dc23
                                    2014049446

Manufactured in the United States of America

CPSIA Compliance Information: Batch #WS15PK: For Further Information contact Rosen Publishing, New York, New York at 1-800-237-9932

CONTENTS

WAITING IN YOUR BED

When people go to sleep, bugs might be waiting in their bed to feed on them! These bugs are called bedbugs because they're most commonly found in or near people's beds.

Bedbugs are parasites, which means they feed on the bodies of other animals. A bedbug's favorite meal is human blood. These bugs feed by biting people while they sleep. This is why bedbugs are found where people sleep, such as bedrooms, apartments, and even fancy **hotels**.

These bedbugs are waiting for a person to fall asleep on this bed. Then, they'll be able to eat!

A CLOSER LOOK

Adult bedbugs are small. They're only around 0.2 to 0.28 inch (5 to 7 mm) long. Their bodies are reddish brown and look like flat ovals. If a bedbug has eaten recently, its flat body is bigger and looks more like a balloon. This is because its body is now full of human blood.

Bedbugs have two antennae, or feelers. Unlike many other bugs, bedbugs don't have wings. They don't fly to get from place to place.

FREAKY FACT!

BEDBUGS STINK! THEY HAVE SPECIAL BODY PARTS CALLED SCENT GLANDS THAT PRODUCE A SWEET, **MUSTY** SMELL.

A bedbug's small, flat body helps it hide as it travels from place to place on things such as bedding and clothing.

A BEDBUG'S LIFE CYCLE

An adult bedbug is in the final **stage** of its life cycle. Like most bugs, bedbugs begin their life cycle as an egg. Female bedbugs can lay as many as 500 eggs in their lifetime.

The next stage in a bedbug's life cycle is the nymph stage. Nymphs are young bedbugs that are smaller than adults. A bedbug goes through five different nymph stages before it becomes an adult. It molts, or loses its skin, as it goes through each stage.

BEDBUG SKIN

LIFE CYCLE OF A BEDBUG

EGG
- the size of a pinhead
- white

NYMPH
- smaller than adult
- clear or whitish yellow
- molts five times before becoming an adult

ADULT
- 0.2 to 0.28 inch (5 to 7 mm) long
- reddish brown
- females lay eggs

Bedbugs look very different at each stage of their life cycle.

THEY NEED TO FEED

Bedbug nymphs need to molt before they can move on to the next stage of their life cycle. They also need to eat. Bedbug nymphs must have at least one meal of blood before they can go from one stage to the next. They can, however, eat more than once before moving on to the next stage.

Adult bedbugs also need to eat in order to mate, or make babies. They have to eat at least once every 14 days to make new bedbugs.

FREAKY FACT!

BEDBUGS DON'T HAVE TO EAT VERY OFTEN TO STAY ALIVE. THEY CAN SOMETIMES GO MONTHS OR EVEN A YEAR WITHOUT EATING HUMAN BLOOD!

This bedbug nymph is feeding on a person's blood. It needs to do this in order to grow into an adult bedbug.

WHERE DO THEY LIVE?

Human blood is needed to keep bedbugs alive, so bedbugs live wherever people do. They're found all over the world. Bedbugs don't care if a place is clean or dirty. They can be found in even the cleanest homes and hotels.

Because bedbugs like to feed on sleeping people, they're often found in beds. They can also be found in places near beds, such as behind wallpaper and hiding under and around objects in a bedroom.

BEDBUG ADULTS AND NYMPHS ON HEADBOARD OF BED

Some dogs are trained to find bedbugs near beds
by using their sense of smell.

TIME TO EAT!

Bedbugs eat at night and hide during the day. They travel from their hiding places to find a human host. A host is an animal a parasite feeds on.

Because bedbugs are so small, they can't hold a lot of human blood. As they eat fresh blood, old blood comes out of their body as waste to make more room. You can see this old blood on bedsheets. It looks like rust-colored spots.

FREAKY FACT!

WHEN A BEDBUG BITES A PERSON, IT **NUMBS** THE SPOT WHERE IT BITES. THIS MEANS A PERSON WON'T KNOW THEY'VE BEEN BITTEN UNTIL THE BITE MARKS SHOW UP LATER.

Bedbugs change color when they eat. They turn
redder because human blood is red.

BEDBUG BITES

People who are bitten by bedbugs often see bite marks afterward. These marks can take up to two weeks to appear, and sometimes they don't show up at all. The bites generally look like **mosquito** bites. They're slightly **swollen**, red areas on a person's skin. These areas may be **itchy**, and the itching can make people lose sleep.

Bedbugs don't carry sicknesses like many other parasites. Their bites might make you itch, but they won't make you sick.

FREAKY FACT!

SOME PEOPLE ARE **ALLERGIC** TO BEDBUG BITES. THIS MEANS BITE MARKS ON THEIR SKIN MIGHT BECOME PAINFUL, AND THEY MIGHT HAVE TROUBLE BREATHING AFTER BEING BITTEN.

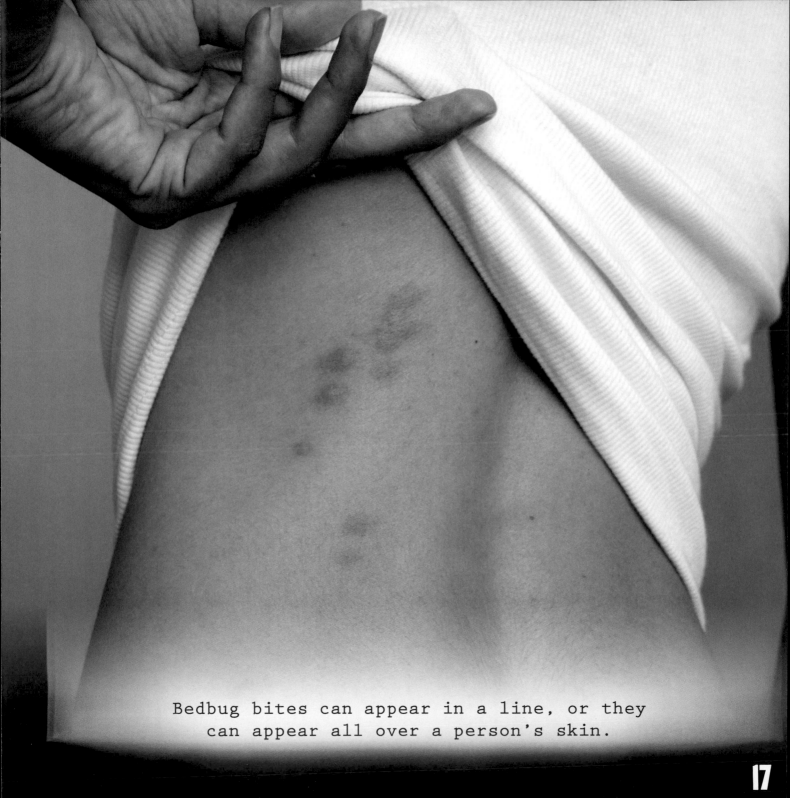

Bedbug bites can appear in a line, or they can appear all over a person's skin.

LOOKING FOR BEDBUGS

If you ever wake up covered in itchy bug bites, you should check for signs of bedbugs. The first step to getting rid of these parasites is finding them!

Sometimes you can see actual bedbugs in your bed, but there might also be red spots of old blood left behind as waste. You might also find bedbug eggs or the skins left behind by nymphs as they grow. Checking for signs of bedbugs is a good way to keep from getting bitten.

FREAKY FACT!

BECAUSE BEDBUGS HAVE A SWEET AND MUSTY SCENT, YOU MIGHT ALSO BE ABLE TO FIND THEM BY USING YOUR NOSE!

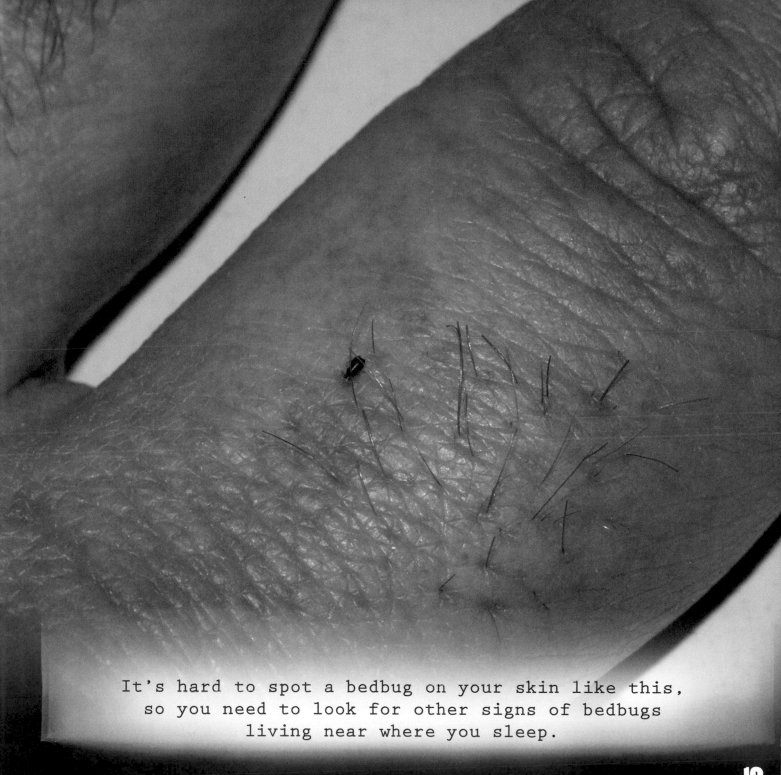

It's hard to spot a bedbug on your skin like this, so you need to look for other signs of bedbugs living near where you sleep.

NO MORE BEDBUGS!

Bedbugs are pesky parasites, and no one wants to wake up with bedbug bites. People have come up with many different ways to get rid of these bugs. Bedbugs can't live if it's very cold or very hot. One way to try to get rid of bedbugs is to put sheets with bedbugs on them in the dryer. That makes it too hot for bedbugs to live on the sheets.

Other people use bug-killing **chemicals** called pesticides to get rid of bedbugs. Pesticides can hurt people, too. They need to be used very carefully.

Pesticides are often used by people whose job is to kill bugs such as bedbugs. These people are called exterminators.

PESKY PARASITES

Bedbugs seem scary. They generally feed on human blood every five to 10 days. However, bedbugs aren't a real danger to people who aren't allergic to them because they don't carry sicknesses.

It's important to check for bedbugs if you think they might be living near you or if you're sleeping in a new place. This might save your blood from becoming a bedbug's next meal!

GLOSSARY

allergic: Having a medical condition that causes someone to become sick after coming into contact with something that is harmless to most people.

chemical: Matter made by mixing two or more different kinds of matter together.

hotel: A place that has rooms in which paying guests can stay, especially while traveling.

itchy: Producing an unpleasant feeling on your skin that makes you want to scratch.

mosquito: A small, flying bug. Female mosquitoes have a pointed body part used for sucking the blood of humans and other animals.

musty: Having a bad smell because of wetness, old age, or lack of fresh air.

numb: To make someone or something unable to feel.

stage: A step in the growth of a living thing.

swollen: Made larger than normal.

INDEX

WEBSITES

Due to the changing nature of Internet links, PowerKids Press has developed
an online list of websites related to the subject of this book. This site is updated
regularly. Please use this link to access the list: www.powerkidslinks.com/bfp/bed